EIGHTH NOTE ♪ PUBLICATIONS

The Haunting of Keg Mansion

Ryan Meeboer

Keg Mansion, formerly known as Euclid Hall, is located on Jarvis Street in Toronto, Canada. This famous mansion was originally built for Arthur McMaster and later purchased by the Massey family. In 1976, the Keg Steakhouse restaurant chain purchased the mansion, hence the name, Keg Mansion. Over the years, many have claimed sightings of ghosts in the restaurant, including the sounds of children playing on the stairs and a spirit in the woman's washroom on the second floor.

The Haunting of Keg Mansion opens by setting up the chilling sensation of a haunted mansion: dark harmonies and powerful dynamics. The main melody is quick and fidgety, much like that of a mischievous presence. The haunting setting continues with the striking chords in the middle contrasting section of the piece. Be sure these chords are played powerfully, but in control of tone.

Ryan Meeboer is a music educator, who obtained his degree through the Ontario Institute for Studies in Education at the University of Toronto. As a composer, he has written and arranged many pieces for concert band, jazz band, and small ensembles. His young band piece, *Last Voyage of the Queen Anne's Revenge*, has been well received by performers, educators, and audiences, and his pieces are starting to be found on festival and contest lists. As a performer, he has had experience in several groups, including concert and stage bands, chamber choir, vocal jazz ensemble, acoustic duets, and the Hamilton based swing group, "The Main Swing Connection".

Ryan began studying music at the age of seven through private guitar lessons. During his years in elementary and secondary school, he gained experience in several families of instruments. Focusing on music education and theory (including composition and orchestration), he attended McMaster University to achieve his honours degree in music. Ryan is currently a teacher for the Halton District School Board in Ontario, where he continues to compose and arrange.

Please contact the composer if you require any further information about this piece
or his availability for commissioning new works and appearances.

ryan.meeboer@enpmusic.com

ISBN: 9781771577410
CATALOG NUMBER: BQ220509
COST: $15.00
DURATION: 2:00
DIFFICULTY RATING: Easy
Brass Quintet

THE HAUNTING OF KEG MANSION

Ryan Meeboer

Bb Trumpet 1

THE HAUNTING OF KEG MANSION

Ryan Meeboer

THE HAUNTING OF KEG MANSION pg. 2

Bb Trumpet 2

THE HAUNTING OF KEG MANSION

Ryan Meeboer

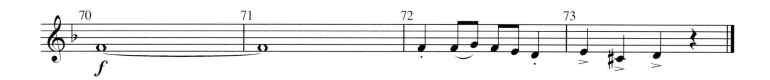

THE HAUNTING OF KEG MANSION pg. 2

F Horn

THE HAUNTING OF KEG MANSION

Ryan Meeboer

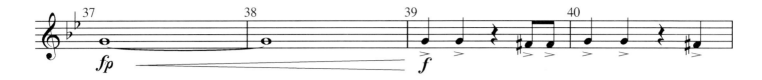

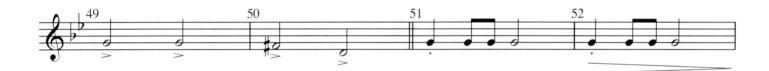

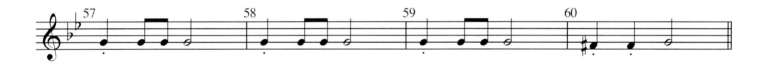

THE HAUNTING OF KEG MANSION pg. 2

Trombone

THE HAUNTING OF KEG MANSION

Ryan Meeboer

THE HAUNTING OF KEG MANSION pg. 2

Tuba

THE HAUNTING OF KEG MANSION

Ryan Meeboer

THE HAUNTING OF KEG MANSION pg. 3